Material Matters
Non-metals

Carol Baldwin

www.raintreepublishers.co.uk
Visit our website to find out more information about **Raintree** books.

To order:
☎ Phone 44 (0) 1865 888113
🗎 Send a fax to 44 (0) 1865 314091
💻 Visit the Raintree Bookshop at **www.raintreepublishers.co.uk** to browse our catalogue and order online.

First published in Great Britain by Raintree Publishers,
Halley Court, Jordan Hill, Oxford, OX2 8EJ, part of
Harcourt Education Ltd.
Raintree is a registered trademark of Harcourt
Education Ltd.

© Harcourt Education Ltd 2005
First published in paperback in 2005
The moral right of the proprietor has been asserted.

Produced for Raintree Publishers by Discovery
Books Ltd.
Editorial: Louise Galpine, Carol Usher, Charlotte Guillain,
and Isabel Thomas
Design: Victoria Bevan, Keith Williams
(sprout.uk.com Limited), and Michelle Lisseter
Picture Research: Maria Joannou and Alison Prior
Production: Duncan Gilbert and Jonathan Smith
Originated by Dot Gradations Ltd
Printed and bound in China
by South China Printing Company

ISBN 1 844 43357 9 (hardback)
09 08 07 06 05
10 9 8 7 6 5 4 3 2 1

ISBN 1 844 43620 9 (paperback)
09 08 07 06 05
10 9 8 7 6 5 4 3 2 1

British Library Cataloguing in Publication Data
Baldwin, Carol 1943-
Non-metals – (Freestyle express. Material matters)
1. Nonmetals – Juvenile literature
546.7

A full catalogue record for this book is available from the
British Library.

This levelled text is a version of
Freestyle: Material Matters: Non-metals.

Photo acknowledgements
p.4/5, Robert Harding/N Wheeler; p.5 bottom Science Photo
Library; p.5 middle, Photodisc /Getty; p.5 top, NASA/
Kennedy Space Center; p.6, Art Directors Trip/A Lambert; p.7
left, Science Photo Library/ Claude Nuridsany & Marie
Perennou; p.7 right, Robert Harding/ Greg Johnston; p.8, Art
Directors & Trip/; p.10, Aspect Picture Library/B Davis;
p.10/11, Hutchison Library; p.8/9, p.11, p.33 right, Corbis;
p.12, 34 left, 41, Trevor Clifford; p.13, Science Photo
Library/Andrew Syred; p.14, Photodisc /Getty; p.14/15,
NASA/SOHO; p.15, Illustrated London News; p.16, Trevor
Clifford; p.16/17, Corbis/ Bettmann; p.17, Getty Images/
Photodisc; p.18 left, Art Directors & Trip/W Jacobs; p.18
right, NASA/ Kennedy Space Center; p.19, Science Photo
Library; p.20, Science Photo Library/Volker Steger; p.20–21,
p.44/45, Corbis/D. Boone; p.22 bottom, Science Photo
Library/Peter Menzel; p.22 top, Science Photo Library/Dr Tim
Evans; p.23, Robert Harding Picture Library/Phototake; p.24,
Camera Press/Femina; p.24/25, FLPA/Celtic Picture Library;
p.25, Tudor Photography p.26, Science Photo Library/Adam
Hart-Davis; p.26/27, Digital Vision; p.27, Art Directors &
Trip; p.28, Tudor Photography; p.28/29, FLPA/Alwyn/
Roberts p.29, Science Photo Library/David Taylor; p.30,
Science Photo Library/ Eye of Science; p.30/31, ImageState;
p.31, 32, 35, 39 Getty Images/ Photodisc; p.33 left, NASA;
p.34 right, Art Directors & Trip/A Lambert; p.36, Art
Directors & Trip/Beanstalk Images; p.36–37, Corbis/F
Wartenberg ; p.37, Hulton Archive; p.38 left, Art Directors &
Trip/A Lambert; p.38 right, Corbis/S Adey; p.40, Corbis/R
White; p.40/41, Science Photo Library/ George Post; p.42,
Corbis/R Ressmeyer; p.42/43, Corbis/David Brooks; p.43,
Science Photo Library/ National Cancer Institute.

Cover photograph of crystals of quartz (a silicon compound)
reproduced with permission of Science Photo Library/
Lawrence Lawry.

Every effort has been made to contact copyright holders of any
material reproduced in this book. Any omissions will be rectified
in subsequent printings if notice is given to the Publishers.

Contents

Any words appearing in the text in bold, **like this**, are explained in the Glossary. You can also look out for some of them in the Word bank at the bottom of each page.

Non-metals everywhere

When we take a deep breath, our lungs fill with air. Air is a mixture of gases. All the gases belong to a group called non-metals. Not all non-metals are gases. Some are solids and one is a liquid at **room temperature**.

Non-metals

Non-metals do not let heat or electricity pass through them easily. Solid non-metals are dull and are easy to break. Non-metals have the opposite properties to metals.

Gases in air

Some gases in air are pure non-metals. Others are made up of two or more non-metals. These have combined together. Then they are called **compounds**.

- 78% nitrogen
- 21% oxygen
- 0.9% argon
- 0.1% other gases.

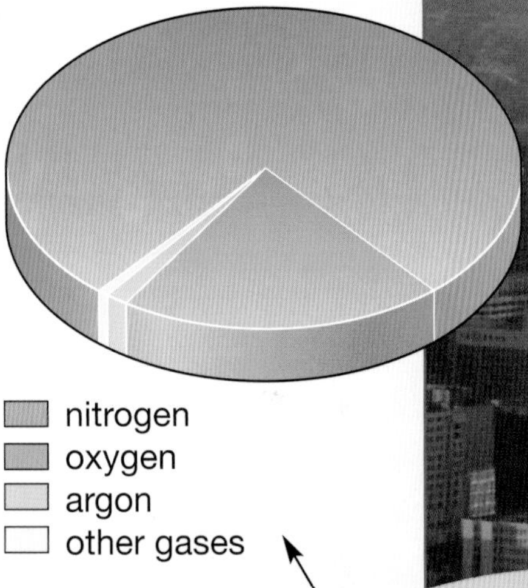

- nitrogen
- oxygen
- argon
- other gases

This chart shows the different non-metals in air.

This is Los Angeles. Sometimes the air is brown. Non-metals are to blame for this.

Word bank   room temperature about 20 °C (68 °F)

Non-metals in our bodies

The human body is mostly made up of non-metals. The main ones are:

- 65 per cent oxygen
- 10 per cent hydrogen
- 18 per cent carbon
- 3 per cent nitrogen

Find out later ...

... which non-metal is used as rocket fuel.

... which non-metal is made by plants.

... how to see if a dangerous non-metal is in your home.

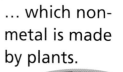

compound substance made of two or more different
elements joined together

Properties of non-metals

Non-metals can be solids, liquids, or gases. Most non-metals are gases at **room temperature**.

The non-metal gases are:

• hydrogen	• fluorine	• krypton
• helium	• chlorine	• xenon
• nitrogen	• neon	• radon
• oxygen	• argon	

These non-metals are solids at room temperature:

• carbon	• sulphur	• astatine
• phosphorus	• iodine	

There is only one non-metal that is a liquid at room temperature. It is bromine.

Some non-metals block out light

Only some solid non-metals are **opaque**, like sulphur and **graphite**. All metals are opaque. This means light cannot pass through them.

Chlorine
Carl Wilhelm discovered chlorine in 1774. Chlorine is a yellow gas at room temperature. It is poisonous and has a choking smell.

Word bank   opaque (say "oh-PAYK") not letting light pass through

Some non-metals allow light through

Many liquids are **translucent**. Some light can pass through them, but not all. **Diamond** is a solid and a non-metal. It is translucent. **Transparent** substances let light pass through them.

A liquid can be translucent or transparent. Light can pass through a thin layer of water, but not a thick layer. Deep parts of the ocean are pitch black.

This grey-purple solid is iodine. When it is heated, it gives off violet iodine gas.

Dangerous nitrogen

There is a lot of nitrogen gas in air. Usually people breathe it in without a problem. But if scuba divers surface too quickly, bubbles of nitrogen quickly form in their bodies. They can get a sickness called the **"bends"** and can die.

Non-metals have low densities

Density tells us how much there is of something in a certain space. To find the density of a material, you divide its **mass** by its **volume**. The mass of something tells us how much of it there is. Volume is the amount of space an object takes up.

Non-metals have lower densities than metals. Carbon has a low density. The metal, iron, is nearly four times as dense as the non-metal, carbon.

Lighter than air

Airships and party balloons are often filled with helium. They float upwards in the air. This is because helium is less dense than the air.

element substance made from one type of atom

Forming compounds

Compounds are made from two or more **elements** joined together. Water is a compound of two non-metals. Hydrogen and oxygen join to form water.

Non-metals also join with metals like copper, sodium, and iron. Common table salt is a compound of sodium (metal) and chlorine (non-metal).

Diatomic gases
Hydrogen is a **diatomic** gas. Diatomic means a gas has "two **atoms**". Diatomic gases have the same type of atoms or **particles**. The atoms exist in pairs (see diagram below).

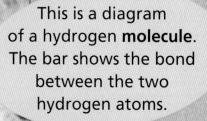

This is a diagram of a hydrogen **molecule**. The bar shows the bond between the two hydrogen atoms.

This "do-nut" is filled with air. It floats because the air is less dense than the water.

atom tiny particle that makes up everything

Silver and sulphur

You can polish silver (a metal) to look shiny. But sulphur (non-metal) will never shine even if you polish hard.

Metals, like silver, can be hammered without breaking. They can also be rolled into sheets and stretched into wires.

Non-metals are brittle

All solid non-metals are **brittle** like **graphite** in a pencil. This means they break easily. They will not bend or stretch like metals do. **Diamond** is another form of carbon. It is used in jewellery. It is tougher than graphite. But when it is hit hard, it will shatter.

Non-metals are dull

Non-metals do not shine like metals, such as gold. Solid non-metals look dull, like graphite.

Non-metals are poor conductors

Heat does not travel quickly or easily through non-metals. They are poor **conductors**. But this means they are usually good **insulators**. They stop heat moving away. Air is a good insulator. Birds fluff up their feathers in cold weather. This traps air between their feathers and stops their body heat from escaping.

Most non-metals do not let electricity pass through them. Graphite is the only one that does. Non-metals, like dry air and carpet, are poor conductors of electricity. They are good insulators.

Copper and phosphorus

Phosphorus (a non-metal) does not conduct heat well. But copper (a metal) does. That is why many cooking pans have copper bottoms.

Sulphur is brittle, like other solid non-metals.

Copper is a good conductor of electricity. Electrical wiring in buildings is usually made of copper wire.

The periodic table

These match heads contain phosphorus. The chemical symbol for phosphorus is P.

Atoms

Everything is made from tiny bits of matter or material, called **atoms**. At the centre of an atom is its **nucleus**. The nucleus contains two types of **particle**. These are **protons** and **neutrons**. Protons have a positive charge. Neutrons have no charge.

Electrons are a third type of particle. They are found in different energy levels or shells around the nucleus. Electrons have a negative charge.

Symbols of elements

Each element has a symbol. These are called chemical symbols. They are a short way of writing the names of the elements. Symbols have one or two letters.

Key

☐	metals
☐	metalloids
☐	non-metals

Example

2 — group number

beryllium — name

Be — symbol

The Transition Metals

1	2							
hydrogen **H**								
lithium **Li**	beryllium **Be**							
sodium **Na**	magnesium **Mg**							
potassium **K**	calcium **Ca**	scandium **Sc**	titanium **Ti**	vanadium **V**	chromium **Cr**	manganese **Mn**	iron **Fe**	cobalt **Co**
rubidium **Rb**	strontium **Sr**	yttrium **Y**	zirconium **Zr**	niobium **Nb**	molybdenum **Mo**	technetium **Tc**	ruthenium **Ru**	rhodium **Rh**
caesium **Cs**	barium **Ba**		hafnium **Hf**	tantalum **Ta**	tungsten **W**	rhenium **Re**	osmium **Os**	iridium **Ir**
francium **Fr**	radium **Ra**		rutherfordium **Rf**	dubnium **Db**	seaborgium **Sg**	bohrium **Bh**	hassium **Hs**	meitnerium **Mt**

Word bank   nucleus centre of an atom that is dense and has a positive charge

Elements

When a substance is made up of just one type of **atom** it is called an **element**. There are over a hundred different kinds of elements. Sometimes different types of element join together. These are called **compounds**.

Grouping elements

The elements are arranged in a chart. This is called the **periodic table**. The columns going down are called groups. Elements in the same group have similar **properties**.

All the elements to the right of the stepped line are not metals. Hydrogen is also a non-metal.

Metalloids

Some elements have properties of both non-metals and metals. They are called **metalloids**. Silicon and arsenic are metalloids. They are both used in computer chips.

This silicon chip is so small an ant can carry it.

								0
								helium **He**
			3	4	5	6	7	
			boron **B**	carbon **C**	nitrogen **N**	oxygen **O**	fluorine **F**	neon **Ne**
			aluminium **Al**	silicon **Si**	phosphorus **P**	sulphur **S**	chlorine **Cl**	argon **Ar**
nickel **Ni**	copper **Cu**	zinc **Zn**	gallium **Ga**	germanium **Ge**	arsenic **As**	selenium **Se**	bromine **Br**	krypton **Kr**
palladium **Pd**	silver **Ag**	cadmium **Cd**	indium **In**	tin **Sn**	antimony **Sb**	tellurium **Te**	iodine **I**	xenon **Xe**
platinum **Pt**	gold **Au**	mercury **Hg**	thallium **Tl**	lead **Pb**	bismuth **Bi**	polonium **Po**	astatine **At**	radon **Rn**
darmstadtium **Ds**	roentgenium **Rg**	ununbium **Uub**	ununquadium **Uuq**					

Hydrogen

Hydrogen in the Earth's atmosphere

There is not much hydrogen in the Earth's **atmosphere**. But much of the universe is made out of hydrogen.

Hydrogen

Hydrogen is the simplest of all the **atoms**. It is made of one **proton** and one **electron**. Hydrogen is the most common **element** in the **universe**. It is the main element in all stars.

There are huge amounts of hydrogen in the space between the stars too. About 93 per cent of atoms in the universe are hydrogen atoms.

Out of one million parts of air, only five parts are hydrogen.

The Sun produces enormous amounts of heat and light.

Word bank   atmosphere layer of gases around the Earth

Hydrogen gas

Hydrogen is a **diatomic** gas. This means two **atoms** of hydrogen are joined together. Because of this the symbol for hydrogen gas is H_2.

Hydrogen gas has no smell or taste and it is colourless. Hydrogen is very easily set on fire and produces huge amounts of heat. Hydrogen is the lightest gas. A balloon filled with hydrogen gas will rise and float away when you let it go.

Hydrogen disaster

The *Hindenburg* was a large airship. It was filled with hydrogen. A spark **ignited** the hydrogen. The airship burst into flames and crashed.

This is the *Hindenburg* accident. After this, hydrogen was no longer used in airships.

ignite catch fire

Getting hydrogen from acids

All **acids** contain hydrogen. Hydrogen is produced when an acid **reacts** with a metal. Henry Cavendish was an English chemist. He discovered hydrogen in 1766. He added some zinc metal to an acid and hydrogen was produced.

Hydrogen gas is still made this way. It is easy to test if you have made hydrogen in a test tube. Hold a lighted splint in the mouth of a test tube. The hydrogen burns with a squeaky pop.

Recharge car batteries in a place with plenty of fresh air. It is safer that way.

coke form of carbon made from coal

Hydrogen and water

On Earth, most hydrogen **atoms** are found in water. Two atoms of hydrogen join with one atom of oxygen. This **compound** is water. Water is split apart to make large amounts of hydrogen gas.

Hydrogen is made by passing steam over hot **coke**. The steam and coke react to make a mixture of gases. It is easy to separate the gases. Hydrogen is **compressed** and stored in **cylinders**.

Hydrogen is used to make fertilizers, rocket fuel, and hydrochloric acid.

Water maker
Hydrogen comes from the Greek word *hydro*, meaning "water" and *genes* meaning "forming".

compress squeeze into a tight space

Coal, **natural gas**, and oil were formed from living things. They contain hydrogen too.

Hydrogen compounds

Many compounds are made from hydrogen, carbon, and oxygen. Some of these are sugar and fat. These compounds are found in all living things.

The Space Shuttle carries liquid hydrogen and liquid oxygen in separate tanks.

Word bank   dissolve mix completely and evenly

Hydrogen is used to make ammonia

Ammonia (NH_3) is a **compound** of nitrogen and hydrogen. It is a colourless gas with a strong smell. It easily **dissolves** in water.

Ammonia is used in many cleaning products. It is also used to make **fertilizers** for crops.

Hydrogen is used to get pure metals

Many metals are joined to oxygen when we find them. But the metals need to be separated from the oxygen. We can use hydrogen to get the pure metal. For example, the **chemical reaction** between hydrogen and copper **oxide** forms copper and water.

Hydrogen is used in foods

If you look in the kitchen cupboard you might find sunflower oil. This is a vegetable oil. It is a liquid. This is because the vegetable oil has been treated with hydrogen.

Hydrogen is used as rocket fuel

Liquid hydrogen is used to power the main engines of the Space Shuttle. The hydrogen burns in oxygen to make hot steam. The steam rushes out of the engines. This forces the Shuttle upwards.

Pure power
Soon cars could be powered by **hydrogen fuel cells**. They join hydrogen and oxygen together to make water. At the same time they make electricity. This runs the car's motor.

This car runs on a hydrogen fuel cell. **Water vapour** is the only gas that comes out of the exhaust.

Carbon

Carbon is in the food you eat and the clothes you wear. You will also find it in your pencils. It can be found in expensive jewellery too.

Diamond

Diamond is made up of carbon **atoms**. Diamond has a high **density**. It is the hardest substance known. But if you hit diamond with a hammer it will shatter. It is very **brittle**.

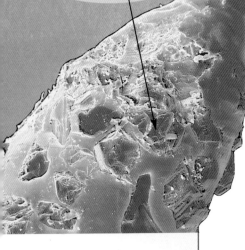

This is a dentist's drill. It is covered in diamonds.

Diamonds and dentists

Diamonds are used for cutting and grinding. Dentists have drills covered in pieces of diamond. They are hard enough to cut through teeth.

buckyball short for buckminsterfullerene; hollow sphere of 60 carbon atoms

Graphite

Another form of carbon is **graphite**. Graphite feels soft and slippery. Graphite is used to help things slide easily, like the tracks of sliding doors.

Coal

Coal is a mixture of carbon and other materials. Coal provides energy for factories and homes. When coal is heated without air, the other compounds burn off. **Coke** is left behind.

Buckyballs

This is a diagram of a **buckyball molecule**. It shows how the carbon atoms (yellow balls) are joined together.

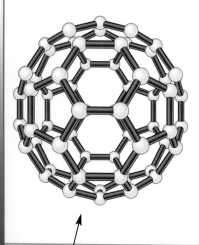

These diamonds are colourless, but they can be different colours. Coloured diamonds can be very valuable.

This diagram shows how the carbon atoms are joined together in a buckyball molecule. They make up the shape of a football.

molecule smallest particle into which a substance can be divided without changing its properties

DNA

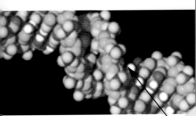

DNA is found in all **cells**. Groups of atoms are lined up in order. This is a code used to make new cells.

Carbon in living things

Proteins are **compounds** that contain carbon. In animals, proteins make up body tissues, like muscle. For our bodies to make proteins we have to eat and **digest** proteins from foods. Meat, fish, and dairy products are good sources of protein.

The coloured units in this diagram are groups of carbon, hydrogen, nitrogen, and phosphorus atoms.

Carbohydrates are made up of carbon, hydrogen, and oxygen. They are a good source of energy for our bodies. Fruits, vegetables, and pasta contain starch and sugar. Starch and sugar are forms of carbohydrates.

This is a fossil of a woolly mammoth. Woolly mammoths lived on Earth about 30,000 years ago. Carbon dating showed us this.

DNA chemical that carries information in the cells of almost all living things

Cooking oils, fat in meat, and butter all contain carbon, hydrogen, and oxygen. Fats help to keep our cells working properly. But eating too many can be harmful.

The remains of this insect are trapped in amber. If the amount of carbon-14 is counted, it can be dated.

Carbon dating

Plants and animals contain carbon. Plants take in carbon in carbon dioxide. They use carbon dioxide to make their own food. Animals take in carbon by eating plants or other animals. Some of these carbon **atoms** are special. They are called carbon-14. Over time carbon-14 atoms change into atoms of other **elements**. This happens one by one.

After a plant or animal dies the amount of carbon-14 starts to drop. Scientists can measure how much carbon-14 is left in a dead plant or animal. From this they can work out how long ago it died. This is called **carbon dating**. It is one way scientists can tell how old **fossils** are.

The dating game
Many things can be dated using carbon. They include:

- wood, twigs, and seeds
- leather (animal skins)
- bone
- charcoal
- hair
- eggshells
- antlers and horns
- fish and insect remains
- seashells.

fossils hard remains of an ancient plant or animal

Carbon dioxide

New carbon dioxide is added to the air all the time. Animals produce carbon dioxide from food in their **cells**. This is added to the air when animals breathe out. **Fossil fuels** such as coal, oil, and gas contain carbon. When they burn, carbon dioxide forms. Volcanoes also give off carbon dioxide.

Luckily plants use up carbon dioxide. They use it to make their own sugars. This helps to balance out the carbon dioxide levels in the air.

Greenhouse effect

The **greenhouse effect** causes the warming up of the Earth's **climate**. Carbon dioxide in the atmosphere stops heat leaving the Earth. In the same way, glass traps heat in a greenhouse.

fossil fuel fuel formed from the remains of plants and animals that lived millions of years ago

Carbon monoxide

Sometimes there is not enough oxygen when carbon burns. If this is the case, **carbon monoxide** forms. Carbon monoxide is a very **poisonous** gas. It has no smell. So carbon monoxide detectors can help save lives. A loud alarm lets people know they are in danger.

Dry ice

Carbon dioxide **freezes** at -78 °C. It is called **dry ice**. When it warms, it changes from a solid into a gas. Unlike real ice there are no messy puddles left when it **melts**.

This power station is burning coal. This adds carbon dioxide to the air.

Dry ice is used to keep foods, like these prawns, frozen when they are shipped.

carbon monoxide poisonous gas produced when carbon burns with not enough oxygen

Nitrogen

Air pollution
Car exhausts release nitrogen **oxides** into the air. In the air, this joins with water, forming nitric **acid**. Drops of this strong acid fall to the Earth when it rains. This is called **acid rain**.

The air around us is made mostly of nitrogen. Nitrogen has no smell, no colour, and no taste. Nitrogen is a **diatomic** gas. Its **atoms** are joined in pairs.

Nitrogen gas does not **react** easily with other **elements** and **compounds**. Even so there are many compounds that contain nitrogen.

Acid rain damages buildings, statues, and living things.

pollution harmful things in the air, water, or land

Producing nitrogen

A huge amount of nitrogen gas is produced each year. Almost all of this comes from air. Air is cooled to a very low temperature until it becomes a liquid. Then it is slowly warmed. As the air warms, each gas **boils** off at a different temperature. Nitrogen turns into a gas at -196 °C. The nitrogen gas is collected in tanks.

Air bag

Car air bags can prevent nasty injuries. When a car crashes, two nitrogen compounds react together. They produce nitrogen gas. This fills the air bag faster than a blink of an eye.

There is a brownish haze over this city. It is caused by air **pollution**. Nitrogen dioxide in the air adds to this.

Car air bags are folded into the steering wheel or the dashboard.

acid rain rain containing nitric acid and sulphuric acid

Nitrogen and living things

All living things need nitrogen. Most living things take nitrogen in through nitrogen **compounds**. Nitrogen gas is in the air. Nitrogen gas is changed to nitrogen compounds by **bacteria** and lightning.

Plants turn nitrogen compounds into **proteins**. Animals eat the plants. They use the plant proteins to make new proteins.

Animals and plants die and rot. Bacteria change the nitrogen compounds from them back into nitrogen gas. This is all part of the nitrogen cycle.

Fresh fruit for longer
Apples, like these, can stay fresh for up to two years in nitrogen. They are put into a sealed room filled with nitrogen gas at a low temperature.

Nitrogen moves between the air, the soil, and living things.

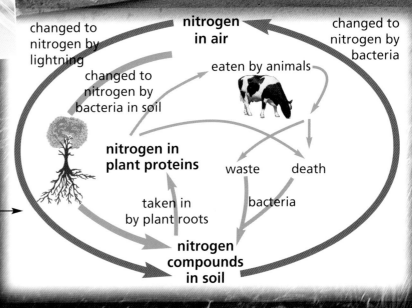

changed to nitrogen by lightning

nitrogen in air

changed to nitrogen by bacteria

changed to nitrogen by bacteria in soil

eaten by animals

nitrogen in plant proteins

waste

death

taken in by plant roots

bacteria

nitrogen compounds in soil

Word bank   bacteria tiny living things that can only be seen under
a microscope

Uses of nitrogen

Crops use up the nitrogen compounds in soil quickly. So farmers add **fertilizers** to the soil. Many fertilizers are made from ammonia. Ammonia is a compound of nitrogen and hydrogen.

Nitric **acid** is a strong acid. It is usually made from ammonia. Nitric acid is used to make explosives and fertilizers. Plastic and nylon are made from nitric acid too.

Other nitrogen compounds are used to help food stay fresh for longer.

Liquid nitrogen

Nitrogen becomes a liquid at -196 °C. That is very cold. As you pour liquid nitrogen, the **water vapour** in the air around it cools too. It changes into droplets of water.

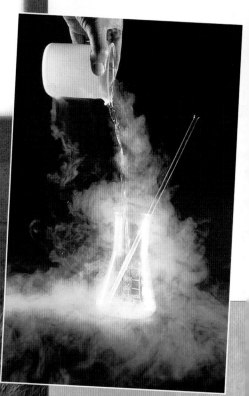

Oxygen

Fruit flies

When you cut up an apple it starts to turn brown quite quickly. This is because oxygen in the air reacts with the fruit. Soon there may be a new product that could stop this. It is a spray made out of fruit flies like this one. Yum!

Oxygen is a **diatomic** gas with no colour, no smell, and no taste. Most oxygen that we use comes from air. To get oxygen, air is cooled until it becomes a liquid. Then it is warmed slowly. Nitrogen and argon boil off, leaving oxygen. It is collected and stored in tanks.

These cows, the grass they are eating, and the trees, need oxygen to release energy.

Word bank   respiration process by which living things use oxygen to produce energy from sugars and give off carbon dioxide

Oxygen and living things

Each time you breathe, you take in oxygen and give out carbon dioxide. Living things, like plants and animals, need oxygen for **respiration**. Respiration takes place in every living **cell**. Sugar and oxygen **react** to form carbon dioxide and water. Energy is released too.

Animals and plants give out the carbon dioxide they make. But plants also use up a lot of the carbon dioxide and produce oxygen. This process is called **photosynthesis**.

Food factories

Plants make their own food! They can do this by photosynthesis. Plants use energy from sunlight. With this they change carbon dioxide gas and water into sugar and oxygen.

photosynthesis process by which green plants use sunlight, water, and carbon dioxide to make their own food

Aeroplane emergency

Above every aeroplane seat is a small container of sodium chlorate and iron. If oxygen is needed, there is a small explosion. This mixes the two chemicals together. They produce oxygen gas.

Oxygen levels can drop on an aeroplane. These masks would help you to breathe in an emergency.

Oxygen compounds

Oxygen joins up with most **elements**. So there are many oxygen **compounds**. Water is the most important oxygen compound. It is made up of oxygen and hydrogen.

Oxides

Oxygen is found in many rocks and **minerals**. Most of the oxygen is in compounds called **oxides**. An oxide is made up of oxygen and another **element**. Many oxides, such as iron oxide, are **ores**. We get important metals from ores. Some oxides are gases, like carbon dioxide.

mineral non-living solid material from the Earth

Ozone

Oxygen **atoms** can join together in groups of three. This form of oxygen is called ozone. Ozone has a blue colour and a strong smell. Ozone can be made when electricity passes through air. For example when lightning strikes.

There is a layer of ozone around the Earth. This stops most of the Sun's harmful rays reaching the Earth's surface. Without the ozone layer most living things on the Earth would be killed.

This satellite photo shows there is a dark area over the South Pole. This means there is very little ozone there.

This runner's face mask contains chemicals that absorb ozone.

Bad ozone
Ozone is not always a good thing. Car exhausts give off ozone. Ozone causes **pollution** when it is near the ground. It can harm people's lungs when they breathe it in.

ore metal that is combined with other elements

Phosphorus and sulphur

Phosphorus

All living things need phosphorus. It is in our bones and teeth and in **DNA**. DNA carries information in **cells**. There are three forms of phosphorus: white, red, and black.

White phosphorus is a white, waxy solid. If you put white phosphorus under **pressure**, black phosphorus forms. This is a black, flaky solid. Above 35 °C white phosphorus bursts into flames. It forms red phosphorus. Red phosphorus is a dark red powder. It is not as **reactive** as white phosphorus.

A phosphate is a **compound** of phosphorus, oxygen, and another **element**.

Safety matches
The striking strip on safety matches contains red phosphorus. When you strike a match, some red phosphorus changes to white phosphorus. The white phosphorus bursts into flame. This makes the matchstick burn.

Phosphorus

hly Flammable   Toxic

White phosphorus catches fire easily and is **poisonous**.

DNA chemical that carries information in the cells of almost all living things

Sulphur

Sulphur is a **brittle**, yellow solid. It burns with a blue flame. Sulphur is often found at the edges of volcanoes. There are also underground **deposits** of sulphur in the USA, Mexico, and Poland.

Sulphur and its compounds are used in many things, like fireworks and paints. Sulphur dioxide can keep some foods fresh.

Most sulphur is used to make sulphuric **acid**. **Fertilizers** are made from sulphuric acid. It is also found in car batteries.

Sulphur in space

Io is one of Jupiter's moons. It has many active volcanoes. In places Io appears yellow. This is because of sulphur. The sulphur comes from the volcanoes.

pressure force on a certain area

Halogens

There are five **elements** in group 7 of the **periodic table**. They are called the **halogens**. The halogens are all non-metals. They are fluorine, chlorine, iodine, bromine, and astatine.

Fluorine

Fluorine is a pale yellow gas. Fluorine **reacts** easily. It always joins up with other elements and forms **compounds**. These are called fluorides. Most fluorine is found in **minerals**, in the Earth's **crust**. Fluorine is also present in seawater and our bodies. Fluorine is used to make the non-stick surfaces of frying pans and artificial valves for hearts.

Saving teeth

In some areas small amounts of sodium fluoride are added to the drinking water. This compound makes teeth stronger.

Fluorides are added to many toothpastes.

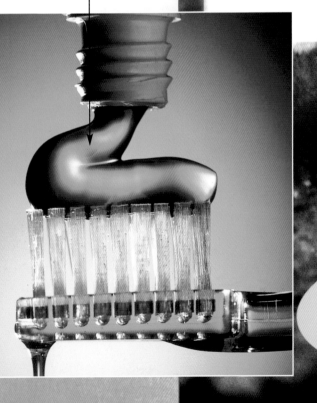

Chlorine in water kills bacteria. It helps keep water safe in swimming pools.

mineral non-living solid material from the Earth

Chlorine

Chlorine is a yellow-green gas. It is very **poisonous**. Chlorine is mostly found as sodium chloride, or common salt.

Chlorine has a choking smell. Chlorine compounds are used to kill **bacteria** in swimming pools and drinking water. Chlorine compounds are used to whiten flour and paper. PVC plastic contains chlorine. This plastic is used to make things from bicycle seats to garden hoses.

Gas attacks

During World War I in Europe, chlorine was used as a poison gas. The first attack was on 22 April 1915.

Three months after the first chlorine gas attack in World War I, soldiers were given gas masks.

Preventing fires

Some bromine compounds prevent fires spreading. They are put in the plastic cases of computer monitors and TV sets. They are also used in fabric coverings for chairs, sofas, and mattresses.

Iodine

Iodine is another **halogen**. Iodine is a shiny, greyish-violet solid. It changes straight from a solid into a violet gas when it is heated. Iodine is found naturally in seaweed, seawater and in some **minerals**. Iodine **compounds** are called iodides.

> Water can be treated with iodine to make it safe to drink.

> This flask is full of bromine gas.

pesticide chemical used to kill harmful insects or animals

We need iodine to keep us healthy. Table salt and animal feeds often contain small amounts of sodium iodide. This makes sure people and animals get enough iodine. But in larger amounts iodine is a poison. Iodine kills **bacteria**. It is mixed in alcohol and used to clean cuts. Silver iodide is used to make film for cameras.

Bromine

Bromine is a reddish liquid. It easily turns into a thick, red-brown gas. Bromine has a sharp, stinging smell. It is very **poisonous** and would burn your skin. If you breathe in its gas, it would damage your nose and throat.

Bromine is found in some minerals, seawater, and salt **deposits**. Bromine compounds are called bromides. They are used for making black and white film and **pesticides**.

Astatine

There are only a few grams of astatine on the Earth at any one time. It is very rare and very little is known about it. But we do know it is **radioactive**.

This sign warns us that radioactive materials are in the container.

Noble gases

The noble gases are on the far right side of the **periodic table**. They are helium, neon, argon, krypton, xenon, and radon. The noble gases have no colour or smell. They rarely join up with other **elements** to make **compounds**. That is why they are called noble gases.

Helium

There is not much helium on the Earth. But there is a lot in the **universe**. On the Earth, most helium is found in **natural gas**.

Heliox
Deep sea divers often breathe a mixture of helium and oxygen. This is called heliox. It prevents them from getting the **"bends"**.

Deep sea divers get high-pitched voices when they breathe heliox.

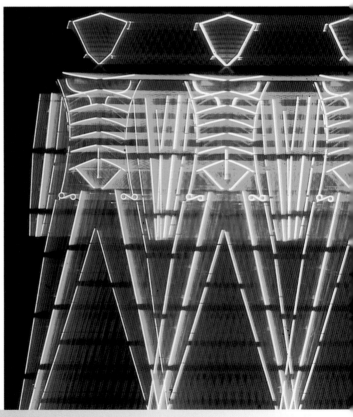

natural gas gas found underground

Helium is less dense than air. This means that balloons filled with helium will rise up in the air and float away.

Neon

Neon is the fifth most common gas in the air. Neon is used with helium in lasers. These are used to read the barcodes on food labels. Neon is also used in bright orange-red advertizing signs.

Argon

Argon makes up almost one per cent of the air. Argon is used in purple advertizing signs. But the argon in light bulbs does not glow purple; it is not hot enough.

A bright idea
Argon-filled light bulbs last much longer than air-filled ones. This is because argon does not **react** with the filament inside the light bulb, like oxygen does.

Neon signs, like this one, usually contain more than one noble gas. Each noble gas produces a different colour.

Krypton

There is very little krypton in the Earth's **atmosphere**. Only a few krypton **compounds** have ever been made.

Krypton, like other noble gases, is used in lights. It is also used in flash lamps. These are used for high-speed photography. Landing strips at airports are lit by krypton lights.

First noble gas compound

In 1962, Neil Bartlett made a compound of xenon. He got it to join up with platinum and fluorine. It was a yellow-orange solid.

This is the Argonne National Laboratory, near Chicago, USA. Scientists made xenon compounds here in the 1960s.

Xenon

Air contains only very tiny amounts of xenon. Xenon gives off a bright white light. Sometimes it is mixed with krypton and used in photographic flash bulbs.

Radon

Radon is a **radioactive** gas. If you breathe it in, it could damage your lungs. Radon can seep into homes from the ground. People who live in homes like this can get lung cancer.

Testing for radon

Test kits are used to find out if a home has a radon problem. Homes with radon problems can be fixed.

These devices are used to measure radon.

Xenon is used in flash bulbs. Photographers use these to take action shots, like this.

Find out more

Websites

BBC Science
News, features, and activities on science.
www.bbc.co.uk

Creative Chemistry
Fun, practical activities, quizzes, puzzles, and more.
www.creative-chemistry.org.uk

skoool.co.uk
Help with science projects and homework.
http://kent.skoool.co.uk

Books

Material World: Materials Technology, Robert Snedden (Heinemann Library, 2001)
Materials All Around Us, Robert Snedden (Heinemann Library, 2001)
Oxygen, Jean F. Blashfield (Raintree, 1999)
Science Files: Glass, Plastics, Steve Parker (Heinemann Library, 2001)

World Wide Web

To find out more about non-metals you can search the Internet. Use keywords like these:

- non-metals +discovery
- radon +UK
- (name of a non-metal) +properties
- elements +"periodic table"

You can find your own keywords by using words from this book. The search tips opposite will help you find useful websites.

Search tips

There are billions of pages on the Internet. It can be difficult to find exactly what you are looking for. These tips will help you find useful websites more quickly:

- know what you want to find out about

- use simple keywords

- use two to six keywords in a search

- only use names of people, places or things

- put quote marks around words that go together, for example "periodic table"

Where to search

Search engine
A search engine looks through millions of website pages. It lists all the sites that match the words in the search box. You will find the best matches are at the top of the list, on the first page.

Search directory
A person, not a computer, has sorted a search directory. You can search by keyword or subject and browse through the different sites. It is like looking through books on a library shelf.

Glossary

acid compound that has a sour taste and will burn you

acid rain rain containing nitric acid and sulphuric acid

atmosphere layer of gases around the Earth

atom tiny particle that makes up everything

bacteria tiny living things that can only be seen under a microscope

bends when a diver comes up too quickly from a dive, bubbles of nitrogen can form in the blood, causing cramps and sometimes death

boil change rapidly from a liquid into a gas

brittle firm to touch but easy to break

buckyball short for buckminsterfullerene; hollow sphere of 60 carbon atoms

carbohydrate compound that contains carbon, hydrogen, and oxygen

carbon dating way of working out how long ago a plant or animal died

carbon monoxide poisonous gas produced when carbon burns with not enough oxygen

cell building block that makes up all living things

chemical reaction change that produces one or more new materials

climate type of weather a place has

coke form of carbon made from coal

compound substance made of two or more different elements joined together

compress squeeze into a small space

conductor material through which heat or electricity passes easily

crust outer layer of the Earth

cylinder storage container that is shaped like a tube

density mass in a certain volume of something

deposit layer of a substance underground

diamond form of carbon that lets some light through and is very hard

diatomic when two of the same type of atom are joined together

digest break down food into small molecules

dissolve mix completely and evenly

DNA chemical that carries information in the cells of almost all living things

dry ice frozen carbon dioxide

electron tiny particle outside the nucleus of an atom with a negative charge

element substance made from one type of atom

fertilizer chemicals added to soils to help plants grow better

fossil hard remains of an ancient plant or animal

fossil fuel fuel formed from the remains of plants and animals that lived millions of years ago

freeze change from a liquid into a solid

graphite form of carbon used in pencils

greenhouse effect warming of the Earth's climate caused by more carbon dioxide in the air

halogen group of non-metal elements in the periodic table

hydrogen fuel cell similar to a battery, but will not run down or need recharging as long as hydrogen is supplied

ignite catch fire

insulator material that stops the flow of heat or electricity

mass amount of matter in an object

melt change from a solid to a liquid

metalloid element that has properties of both metals and non-metals

mineral non-living solid material from the Earth

molecule smallest particle into which a substance can be divided without changing its properties

natural gas gas found underground

neutron particle with no charge, found in the nucleus of an atom

nucleus centre of an atom that is dense and has a positive charge

opaque (say "oh-PAYK") not letting light pass through

ore metal that is combined with other elements

oxide compound of oxygen and another element

particle small part of something

periodic table chart in which elements with similar properties are arranged in groups

pesticide chemical used to kill harmful insects or animals

photosynthesis process by which green plants use sunlight, water, and carbon dioxide to make their own food

poisonous having harmful effects

pollution harmful things in the air, water, or land

pressure force on a certain area

property feature of something

protein large compound that contains nitrogen; used for growth and repair in the body

proton particle in the nucleus of an atom with a positive charge

radioactive gives off particles or rays and changes to a different element

react produce one or more new substances

respiration process by which living things use oxygen to produce energy from sugars and give off carbon dioxide

room temperature about 20 °C (68 °F)

translucent some light can pass through

transparent allows all or most light through

universe everything that we know

volume amount of space something takes up

water vapour water in a gas state

Index